OLIVER CROMWELL
AND
THE BATTLE OF GAINSBOROUGH
JULY 1643

by

JOHN WEST

19 92

RICHARD KAY
80 SLEAFORD ROAD • BOSTON • LINCOLNSHIRE • PE21 8EU

The right of John West to be considered as the author of this work is hereby asserted in accordance with the provisions of the Copyright, Designs, and Patents Act 1988

© John West
ISBN 0902662 43 0

British Library Cataloguing-in-Publication Data.
A catalogue record for this book is available from the British Library.

Oliver Cromwell – his signature

Typeset on an AppleMacintosh Plus computer
in Bookman10 point typescript for the main body of the text.
Printed and bound by:
Woolnough Bookbinding Ltd. • Express Works • Church Street
• IRTHLINGBOROUGH • Northants • NN9 5SE

DEDICATED TO THE MEMORY OF OLIVER CROMWELL

*'That slovenly fellow which you see before us . . .
will be one of the greatest men of England.'*

John Hampden, M.P. 1640
(pointing out Oliver Cromwell
to a fellow member of Parliament)

CONTENTS

INCLUDING ILLUSTRATIONS

INTRODUCTION

The English Civil War was one of the most bloody conflicts ever fought on British soil. The war raged all over Britain with almost every part of the country becoming involved in one way or another. Battles were fought, towns sacked, and thousands were killed or maimed. In 1643 a battle was fought between Parliament and Royalist forces at the small town of Gainsborough in Lincolnshire. This booklet tells the story of that battle and also something of the man who led the forces for Parliament on that day. . .

CROMWELL LEADS A CHARGE INTO BATTLE

A BRIEF OUTLINE HISTORY OF THE ENGLISH CIVIL WAR

IN 1640 CHARLES 1 had been King for fifteen years. He was a stubborn and arrogant man who believed in 'The Divine Right of Kings' whereby he was answerable only to God himself. Over the years he had frequently clashed with Parliament regarding the way the country was governed and also over the various unjust taxes that he had introduced. In 1629 he finally decided to dissolve Parliament and to rule alone. This later became known as the 'Eleven Years Tyranny'. During these eleven years he again introduced unpopular taxes, such as the notorious 'ship money' in which all towns on the coast had to pay for the upkeep of the Navy. This was later extended to cover inland areas as well, with the money being used by Charles for other purposes which angered the already over taxed population greatly and which helped to make Charles even more unpopular.

In 1637 Charles tried to introduce into Scotland the Anglican Prayer Book, but was met with violent opposition to it. In response to this he ordered his army to march north to quash the rebellion, but his soldiers were defeated and finally in 1640 he had no choice but to recall Parliament to try to get them to raise money for his war with Scotland. If he had hoped to raise the money without Parliament's opposition he was gravely mistaken. Parliament refused to raise taxes for the war and, under the member of Parliament, John Pym, attacked the King's overall policies. After a month Charles once more dissolved Parliament and again made plans to attack the Scots, this time using an Irish army mainly consisting of Catholics. But yet again his plans proved disasterous. The Scots invaded England and captured Newcastle, so once again Charles had to recall Parliament after agreeing to pay the Scots army a subsidy of £25,000 per month.

This time Parliament was determined not to be dissolved again and started to draw up various grievances against the King. In 1641 in Ireland, a serious uprising of the Irish Catholics against the English Protestant settlers broke out. Charles asked Parliament to raise money for an army to restore order in Ireland, but Parliament fearing that he might use the army against his enemies in England and Scotland, instead drew up an article condemning royal policy during the entire reign of Charles. Charles decided to arrest John Pym and the four other figures leading the opposition against him. He entered Parliament by force only to find they had escaped. After this, Charles left London and set up his Standard at Nottingham on 22nd August 1642, thus declaring war on Parliament and starting the English Civil War.

Both sides now called to arms and in October at Edgehill in Warwickshire the first major battle of the Civil War began. At this indecisive clash, Oliver Cromwell, a man of 43 years of age, took part as a cavalry officer. No one could have known that this man was to become the most skilful and effective military leader of the war and who was eventually to rule Britain as Lord Protector for five years.

Over the next few years various battles and skirmishes were fought all over Britain, finally ending with the defeat of Charles at the Battle of Naseby in 1645. Charles surrendered to the Scots who gave him over to Parliament who in turn decided to put him on trial for causing the Civil War. In 1649 he was found guilty and executed in Whitehall, London. England was declared a Republic for the first and only time in its history. This Republic was to last until the so-called Restoration of 1660.

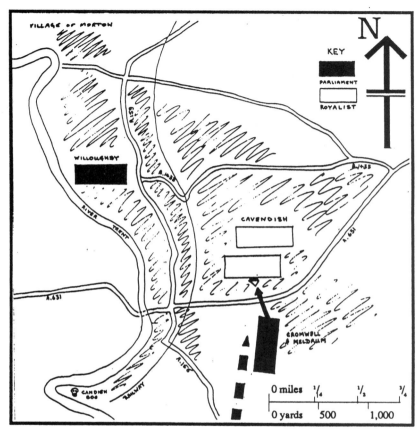

THE BATTLE OF GAINSBOROUGH

July 1643

Shown in relation to the modern town.
The map is approximately to scale. The built up area of the modern town is indicated by the shading. In the Civil War period the town would have extended no further east than the modern A159.

GAINSBOROUGH

AND

THE CIVIL WAR

THE FIRST RECORDED reference to Gainsborough as a settlement is in the Anglo-Saxon Chronicle of 1013, although it is safe to assume that before this prehistoric and Roman settlers would have found the fertile land to the east of the River Trent suitable for habitation and farming. After the departure of the Roman legions in 407, Saxon immigrants gradually began to settle in the area and their first settlement would probably originally have consisted of a small farm surrounded by a wooden stockade and ditch.

The name of Gainsborough probably originates from this time and is taken from the word Burh, meaning fortified settlement and Gainas, which was probably the name of the owner.

As the Saxons finally gained supremacy over England various kingdoms began to be established and Gainsborough found itself lying at a strategic crossing of the Trent, on the frontiers of Northumbria and Mercia. Because of its new found importance Gainsborough quickly prospered and the subsequent Viking and Norman invasions brought new settlers and trade to the town.

By the 17th century, Gainsborough had become a successful port, trade, and farming centre with two annual fairs being held which attracted merchants from as far away as London. At the outbreak of the Civil War in 1642, Gainsborough's population consisted of roughly about 1800 people whose trades included butchers, leather workers, textile manufacturers, carpenters, bakers and brewers. The town was approximately triangular in shape and covered an area of about one and a quarter miles from north to south and a quarter of a mile mile from west to east. The centre of the town was sited around the parish church of All Saints and the market place. Apart from the stone church and brick manor house the remainder of the town would have consisted of timber framed buildings which lined the main streets of Bridge Street (then known as 'Cawsey') Silver Street, Lord Street, and Market Street.

When Civil War was declared, Gainsborough lay in an area which supported Parliament. There is some evidence to suggest that the town itself had Royalist sympathies although, in the end, the town's inhabitants decide to remain neutral. The town was of strategic importance to both sides, sited as it was on a crossing of the Trent and laying on a crossing of important roads leading south and north. It became obvious that the town would be sought after by both sides and so, in early 1642 a committee was formed for the protection of the town, and earthwork banks and ditches were constructetd for its defence, these still being visible up to the beginning of the last century.

In March 1643, the Royalists decided to act, a raiding party from the Royalist base at Newark was sent by Sir John Henderson to capture Gainsborough for the King. In the early morning the town was surrounded and the Royalists demanded surrender. This was quickly done without a shot being fired and without the least resistance. The town was then put into the charge of the Earl of Kingston and was used as a base, together with Newark, to harass the Parliamentary positions in Lincolnshire as well as threatening the Parliamentary situation at their stronghold at Hull. Parliament could not allow this to continue and the Royalist attacks at Louth and Market Rasen, together with the capture of Parliamentary gunpowder intended for Rotherham, made it clear something had to be done. Parliament decided to send Lord Willoughby of Parham, Commander of the Parliamentary forces in Lincolnshire, who on 16th July launched a surprise attack on the town seizing it before the Commander, Kingston, and his men could call to arms. After the surrender, Kingston was taken under guard by river to Hull, but on the journey the boat came under fire from Royalist soldiers on the bank and, as fire was exchanged, Kingston was hit and killed. Willoughby's triumph at Gainsborough was, however, to be short lived. With the fall of Gainsborough, the Royalists had lost their communications with Newark and so immediately sent out a relieving force under the 23 year old Charles Cavendish to besiege the town. As Lord Willoughby exclaimed: 'The same day I tooke it I was beseaged before night, and there kept in some 10 days before I had any release'.

Parliament ordered the town to be relieved and forces from Nottingham under Sir John Meldrum and Colonel Oliver Cromwell from Cambridgeshire, were sent north to attack Cavendish's forces. Cromwell had only just captured a Royalist stronghold at Burghley House and so rushed north to join Meldrum's forces, taking with him 600 Horse and Dragoons. The two forces met up on 27th July at North Scarle, ten miles south of Gainsborough, where they were joined by a detachment of troops from Lincoln. At 2.00 a.m. the following day, the 1200 strong force marched north. At the village of Lea, a mile and a half outside Gainsborough, they met an advanced guard of Cavendish's regiments consisting of about 100 Horse. This force was engaged and, after a short skirmish, was driven back to Cavendish's main body which was drawn up on the top of a steep hill to the east of the town, now known as Foxby hill; the ensuing battle took place on the hillside overlooking Sandsfield Lane. The Royalists consisted of three regiments of Horse with a further regiment in reserve and, although Cavendish had the strategic advantage, Cromwell and his fellow commanders decided they had no choice but to attack, and so the Lincolnshire troops were ordered to advance up the small tracks leading to the summit. Apart from the steep gradient, their advance was also hampered by the numerous rabbit warrens, and, upon reaching the top they came face to face with the Royalist Horse who were, according to Cromwell, only a musket shot away. As the Lincolners were forming up, Cavendish's Horse attacked, hoping to take them at a disadvantage. Upon seeing this, Cromwell, who was in charge of the Right Wing of Horse, charged to meet Cavendish. What happened next is best described by Cromwell himself: 'We came up Horse to Horse, where we disputed it with our swords and pistols a pretty time, all keeping close order, so that one could not break the other'. This fearsome 'Horse to Horse' fighting continued until finally the Royalist Horse gradually began to fall back, eventually fleeing from the battlefield pursued by the Parliamentary cavalry for some 5 miles or so.

Cavendish, meanwhile, had kept a regiment in reserve and taking advantage of the fact that the Parliamentary horse was gone, launched a counter-attack into the Lincolnshire troops who had remained. The Lincolnshires were thrown back and it seemed that Cavendish might yet win the day. But he had not counted on Oliver Cromwell.

Cromwell had not left in the pursuit of the Royalist cavalry and, in fact, had kept back Major Whalley and a reserve of three troops of Horse to deal with Cavendish's reserve regiment. Upon seeing the attack on the Lincolnshires, Cromwell charged Cavendish's rear. In a later account of the battle, Oliver described what happened next. 'I immediately fell on his rear with my three troops, which did so astonish him that he gave over the chase and would fain have delivered himself from me. But I pressing on forced them down the hill, having good execution of them, and below the hill drove the General with some of his soldiers into a quagmire.' Cavendish was knocked off his horse and killed by a sword thrust in the chest by Oliver's Captain-Lieutenant Berry, and the place where he was killed, to the south of the town near the river, was later known as Candish Bog. There was never anything romantic about civil war battles and in this one we can imagine dead and maimed men and horses littering the hillside. Indeed the names later given to the fields around it, such as Graves Close and Redcoats Field, testify to the slaughter that happened there.

For Parliament it had been a great victory and the credit was largely due to Cromwell's skill as a cavalry leader and indeed, it was after this battle that Oliver's military genius first came to the attention of the country.

Now that the battle was over, Cromwell set about supplying Willoughby with such supplies as food, powder, and ammunition to help Willoughby withstand further siege. While this was being done, Cromwell was informed that a small Royalist force of six troops of Horse and 300 Foot were marching on Gainsborough from the north. As Oliver had no foot soldiers Willoughby supplied him with 600 men and Oliver, thinking that this new enemy was a remainder of the late Cavendish's force not yet engaged, went out to meet them. Cromwell and Meldrum approached them by following the low ridge of hills to the east of the town and, as they neared the village of Morton, they encountered two troops of Horse near a mill. These forces were engaged and were driven back down into the village. Cromwell and Meldrum now pushed on and, upon reaching the summit of the hill (probably Spital Hill) were shocked to see not a small Royalist force but instead an entire Royalist army who were now marching on Gainsborough to retake it for the King. As Cromwell was later to recall: 'We saw in the bottom, about a quarter of a mile from us, a regiment of Foot, after that another, after that the Marquis of Newcastle's own regiment consisting in all of about thirty Foot Colours and a great body of Horse - which indeed was Newcastle's army. Which coming so unexpectedly, put us to new consultations.'

Willoughby's foot soldiers, upon seeing this great force, fell back in disorder to the town, but not before suffering casualties due to some Royalist Horse who got in amongst them. As it would have been suicide to stand and fight or to retreat into the town together with the fact that the men and horses were exhausted by the recent battle, Cromwell ordered a withdrawal. The withdrawal was at first hampered by the number of hedgerows and they fell back half a mile in disorder, until they came to the end of a lane at the far end of a field. Here Cromwell ordered a brilliant manoeuvre, which military historians have cited as a classic example of military tactics and genius. Two rearguard parties of Horse consisting of four troops of Cromwell's regiment and four of the Lincoln troop were sent under Captain Ayscough and Major Whalley to stand firm and retire alternately in order to cover Cromwell's main force. On eight or nine occasions, a handful of men held back the Royalists with the loss of only two men until they finally reached the safety of Lincoln. Cromwell later wrote that is was: 'Equal to any of late times and the Honour of it belonged to Major Whalley and Captain Ayscough.'

Meanwhile, Newcastle was besieging Gainsborough and had set up cannon on the surrounding hills with which he started to fire upon the town. Cromwell pleaded that a force of 2000 be raised to relieve Willoughby otherwise ' . . . You will see Newcastle's army march up into your bowels' (The Eastern Counties). However, this was not done and, back at Gainsborough, Newcastle's cannon had set fire to part of the town. The town's inhabitants now started to harass Willoughby's men and threatened to surrender the town themselves. Finally on 31st July, after a three day siege, Willoughby surrendered on terms, although some Royalists looted and ill-treated the Parliamentarians. Newcastle then turned his forces around and headed north to lay siege to the Parliamentary stronghold at Hull leaving Gainsborough in the command of Colonel St. George. Now Gainsborough was again in Royalist hands raiding parties once more started to harass Parliamentary held areas. In response to this, Parliament sent Cromwell's former colleague, Sir John Meldrum, to retake the town. On 18th December, a small fleet of boats were sent out from Hull and fired upon a

Royalist fort at Burton-on-Stather while Meldrum and a body of Horse attacked it from land. After its capture, the combined force advanced down river and commenced firing on Gainsborough. The town surrendered on 20th December with over 600 prisoners, 500 arms, and nine pieces of ordnance being taken. For four months Meldrum used Gainsborough as a base to attack scattered Royalist pockets and also to attack and capture a 'Royal Fort'. In March 1644, Meldrum evacuated the town destroying its defences, due to the approach of a Royalist army under Prince Rupert writing that 'If Gainsborough had not been razed by my order, the enemy might have found a nest to have hatched much mischief'.

CANNON OF THE CIVIL WAR
It was cannon such as these that caused so much panic in the town during Newcastle's siege.

In May 1644, a Parliamentary army under the command of the Earl of Manchester, retook Gainsborough as it marched north to Marston Moor near York (where Parliament was soon to win a great victory against King Charles's army). Manchester's army quartered around Gainsborough and the town was ordered to pay £80 towards the upkeep of the army by the committee of Lincoln. After Manchester had left, a garrison remained and continued to occupy the town for

A PURITAN IN GAINSBOROUGH
Royalists watch a Gainsborough Puritan with suspicion during their occupation of the town.

some time protecting it from any further Royalist attacks. In 1646 Charles and the Royalists finally surrendered and it must have seemed to the inhabitants that they had seen the last of the war. But, in early 1648, while Charles was still a prisoner, Royalist uprisings sprang up throughout Britain. In Doncaster a Royalist force consisting of 400 Horse and 200 Foot moved on the Isle of Axeholme, and, on 30th June crossed the Trent at Gainsborough moving on to capture Lincoln. Parliament acted quickly and an army, under the command of Sir Henry Cholmeley, marched through Gainsborough to met the Royalist army, and, at Willoughby near Nottingham, they were finally routed and defeated. All over Britain the risings were quickly put down and so Gainsborough, at last, found peace. This must have been a great relief to the town's inhabitants, who, since 1643 had had to put up with garrisons, battles, sieges, lootings, and fire. Now the town could get back to a normal routine of living without fear of warfare and the suffering that it brought them.

OLIVER CROMWELL
His Career

ON THE 25TH APRIL 1599 in Huntingdon, Cambridgeshire, a son was born to Robert and Elizabeth Cromwell. They christened him Oliver. His parents were reasonably well off and his father had been a local member of Parliament and Justice of the Peace and was a distant descendant of Thomas Cromwell, the chief minister to Henry VIII. Little is known of Oliver's early life, although there is a story that when he was a baby staying at his uncle's house, a pet monkey seized Oliver and is said to have carried him up on to the roof. Fortunately, for the Cromwell family and for England, he was safely rescued. Another tradition states that the young Oliver was also known as the 'apple dragon' due to his love of scrumping apples.

In 1604 Oliver was sent to the Free School in Huntingdon where he studied such subjects as English Grammar and Latin. His tutor was a Dr. Thomas Beard, a well known Puritan, who influenced Oliver's religious thinking greatly and this firmly rooted religious conviction was to stay with Oliver for the rest of life. In 1616 Oliver was admitted to Sidney Sussex College at Cambridge which was well known for it's Puritan ideas. He stayed there for a year before leaving upon the death of his father to look after the family estates. In 1618 he headed for London to study law at Lincoln's Inn, where he met Elizabeth Bourchier the daughter of a London merchant. They fell in love and in August 1620 they married before moving back to Huntingdon where they farmed and raised a family. In 1628 Oliver inherited some money from a relative and became the Member of Parliament for Huntingdon, sitting in the 1629 Parliament, where he made his maiden speech. Shortly afterwards Charles I dissolved this Parliament and, back at Huntingdon, Oliver became involved in local politics. In 1630 he became a Justice of the Peace and opposed a Royal Charter which would have limited local participation in the running of the town. He was accused of making 'disgraceful and unseemly speeches' and was forced to withdraw his comments by the Privy Council. Shortly afterwards Oliver and his family moved to St. Ives. but he could not afford to buy his own farm so he had to rent one instead. In 1636 a wealthy uncle died leaving Oliver his estates in Ely and so they moved again and set up home in Ely, where they would stay for 11 years. In 1637 he opposed a royal scheme to drain the surrounding fens because it meant that the local people would have lost their livelihoods by losing their supplies of game-birds and fish stocks. Oliver's opposition was successful and the draining was stopped. Oliver was now a figure of wealth and became greatly respected in Ely because of his support for the common people. Later on he was even to be given the nick-name of 'Lord of the Fens'.

In 1640 Parliament was recalled and Oliver became the Member for Cambridge. This Parliament was dissolved after only a few weeks and Oliver's role in it is not certain. When Parliament was again recalled a few months later, Oliver became actively involved in it, backing the many complaints against Charles I and his Court Advisors. In 1641 a document known as the Grand Remonstrance, was drawn up and presented to Charles by Parliament listing all their grievances against him. Cromwell later said that if this Bill had not been passed by Parliament, he would have sold up and gone to America never to return. After Charles tried to arrest certain members of Parliament, Oliver suggested that a committee meet 'to consider the means to put the Kingdom into a posture of defence.

In August 1642 Charles raised his Standard at Nottingham and civil war began. Oliver was ordered by

CHARLES' STANDARD IS RAISED AT NOTTINGHAM
22 AUGUST 1642.
One report of the time states that Charles passed through
Gainsborough on his way to Nottingham.

Parliament to defend Cambridgeshire, where he raised a troop of cavalry in his home town of Huntingdon and then went on to attack and seize Cambridge castle, forcing the University to surrender and, into the bargain, capturing silver plate intended for Charles and the Royalist cause. In October the Battle of Edgehill was fought, Cromwell taking part in the latter stages of the battle amongst the soldiers 'of the right wing . . . who never stirred from their troops but fought till the last minute'. In fact this first major conflict ended with no clear victor and both sides later claimed victory.

At the beginning of the year 1643, Oliver's cavalry troop was made into a regiment and he was appointed Colonel in the army of the Eastern Association which roughly covered the areas of East Anglia and the East Midlands. During this time, Oliver proved himself a great leader of men and a military genius. He won major victories at Grantham, Gainsborough, and Winceby where he had his horse shot from beneath him. Cromwell's army had proved itself brave and courageous in battle and this was largely due to Oliver's personal supervision of the recruitment and training. He made sure his men's high standards on the battlefield were maintained by constant training and harsh discipline, for instance if a man swore he was fined 12d. (a very considerable sum in those days) or if drunk he was put into the stocks. Oliver also chose his men according to their abilities and skills rather than social rank, which for the time was shocking to many people. Cromwell's reputation spread and a grateful Parliament made him Governor of Ely. He was again promoted in 1644 to Lieutenant-General and Parliamentary victories at Marston Moor 1644, and Naseby 1645, were largely due to his unique skill as a soldier and the recent creation of the 'New Model Army'.

After Naseby, the Royalists were all but finished and Oliver was sent to mop up the last Royalist strongholds. In May 1646 Charles surrendered and Parliament ordered the unpaid army to disband with only a reward of 6 weeks back pay even though they were owed months. The Army was furious and, after much thought, Cromwell took up the army's cause. Parliament and army also started to quarrel as the army wanted a say in how the country was run and so Oliver decided to hold the now imprisoned Charles to be in a better position to negotiate for the army. Parliament immediately ordered Cromwell's arrest and London was taken over by anti-army M.P.s The more moderate M.P.s sought the protection of Cromwell so he moved on London with troops and relieved the city. After this Oliver tried to come to an agreement with Charles. But Charles would not listen to anything Cromwell had to say, still believing that he was answerable only to God. Secretly, Charles was also plotting with the Scots to invade England and tried to play all sides off against each other. Finally Oliver decided to give up all hope of coming to terms and determined to put 'that man of blood', Charles Stuart, on trial for causing the Civil War and the bloodshed that followed.

In May 1648 there were Royalist uprisings in various parts of Britain and Cromwell acted instantly crushing the revolt and defeating the Scots at Preston. Back in London the army petitioned Parliament that Charles be put to trial while those M.P.'s who were against the trial were removed from Westminster by troops. Oliver soon returned from Scotland and on the 20th January the trial began. Arrogant to the last, Charles refused to recognize the court and would not plead. A week later he was found guilty and executed. The

CROMWELL DIRECTS A BATTLE

country was now made a Republic and a Council of State was set up with Oliver as Chairman to govern the country. Now the King was dead, the most pressing need was the situation in Ireland which refused to accept the Republic, or Commonwealth as it was known, and which could also be used as a base to invade England by the Royalists under Charles's son presently exiled in Europe. The Council of State decided to make Cromwell Commander-in-Chief and send him to Ireland to restore order. In August 1649 he set sail. The Irish campaign was a a brilliant success with Oliver's military genius shining through yet again. He marched on to the town of Drogheda and defeated the garrison of 2,000 men, then, marching on to Wexford, where, after an eight day siege, the town fell. By winter Cromwell's army had smashed all Irish resistance with his name enough to strike terror into Irish hearts. Even though many of his troops, including himself, had caught malaria and dysentery. In May 1650 he was recalled to England, leaving his son-in-law, Henry Ireton, in command. The reason why Oliver was recalled was a simple one, the Scots had proclaimed Charles's son King and were preparing to attack England. On Cromwell's return he was hailed as a hero and was again made Commander-in-Chief of an army to invade Scotland. At first Oliver tried to reason with the Protestant Scots but they refused to listen, so Cromwell marched north. The opposing armies finally met at Dunbar on the 3rd September, with Cromwell's forces being outnumbered and with his back to the sea. But once again his military genius triumphed, defeating the Scots soundly and taking over 10,000 prisoners. But even after this humiliating defeat, the Scots still refused to give up the Royalist cause and after Cromwell recovered from an illness, he was again forced to fight. Prince Charles had led an army into England in July so Oliver's army pursued him finally surrounding Charles's forces at Worcester. On 3rd September 1651 Cromwell led his army against Charles and after a long bloody fight, defeated the Royalist army with Charles deciding not to stand and die on the battlefield, but instead to flee to Europe, part of the journey disguised as a maid. Worcester was to be Oliver's last battle and also the end of his military career. In all these years of battles, skirmishes, and sieges, Cromwell was to retire having never lost a battle or experienced defeat. A claim that few military men throughout history can equal.

Now that the Royalist cause had finally been defeated and Ireland and Scotland pacified, Cromwell's next concern was for a stable constitution for England. Since the execution of Charles I, England had been ruled by a Council of State and the so-called Rump Parliament consisting of the remainder of the M.P.'s elected in 1640. This Parliament was very unpopular with the people and the army and it was felt they were unrepresentative of the people and they were constantly arguing amongst themselves about the best way to govern. When Cromwell discovered that this Parliament planned to pass a Bill so that it could stay in power without re-election, he decided to act. He attended the Reading of the Bill and then stood up and made a long speech full of passion about the cause that had been fought for before finally losing his temper and attacking them for being corrupt. He then called in soldiers to clear the house, and upon seeing the mace, the symbol of the Rump's authority, he ordered 'the Bauble' to be taken away. The Rump Parliament was not missed and Oliver decided to select another Parliament consisting of 140 members selected by himself with the advice of the Council of State. He had high hopes for this new body but, once again, it was as divided as the previous 'Rump Parliament' and finally in December 1653 it dissolved itself and gave its power to Cromwell. Oliver was bitterly disappointed that once again a nominated parliament had failed and so finally accepted the proposal to make him Lord Protector of the Commonwealth. He was installed as Lord Protector on the 16th December 1653 in Westminster Hall and was given

THE INAUGURATION OF OLIVER CROMWELL AS LORD PROTECTOR 16 DECEMBER 1653.

Hampton Court and Whitehall Palace as his official residences. Over the next few months, Oliver and his Council introduced many new and just laws and this new system of government worked smoothly. In September 1654 the first of the Protectorate Parliaments were summoned but, as before., Cromwell's plans for a just government were yet again to be frustrated by its quarrelling members and, after five months, Oliver dissolved it. In 1655 a small Royalist uprising , in the west country, was put down and Oliver decided to divide England into 11 areas under the command of Major-Generals to keep law and order. But this soon proved unpopular with the population and when Parliament was recalled in September 1656, the scheme was ended. In

January 1657 an assassination attempt on Oliver was foiled and after this, the second Protectorate Parliament, realizing how important Oliver was to the security of the Nation, decided to offer him more constitutional powers and the title of King. Oliver's answer was: 'I am ready to serve not as a King but as a Constable . . . a good Constable to keep the peace of the Parish'. But Parliament would not give up it's idea and in May 1657, they again presented him with a new petition giving Oliver the right to name his successor. together with new constitutional powers but without the title of King. Finally Oliver decided to accept their proposals and on June 26th Cromwell was again invested as Lord Protector in Westminster Hall. Shortly after this, Oliver planned to reform Parliament and set up a second House similar to the old House of Lords. But the third Protectorate Parliament yet again quarrelled over his reforms and it became so violent that in disgust Oliver dissolved it and decided for the good of the Nation to rule alone.

During the last year of his life Oliver's health deteriorated and the malaria which he had suffered from for many years still bothered him. He was now an old man burdened by greatness and responsibilities to the Commonwealth. In August 1658 Oliver's favourite daughter, Elizabeth, died of cancer. He was grief-stricken and never recovered from the shock and sorrow. Oliver gave up the will to live and was later too ill to attend Elizabeth's funeral. He gradually got worse and on 3rd September, the anniversary of his two greatest victories at Dunbar and Worcester, he died. It was typical of his love for his country that his last prayer was for his Nation and his people. He was given a State Funeral and was laid to rest in Westminster Abbey. When Cromwell died so did the Commonwealth.

His successor, his son Richard, was not strong enough to govern and was not as respected as his father. Eventually, he resigned and on May 30th 1660 Charles II returned. In January 1661 in a vile act of revenge which showed people just the type of things Charles II was capable of, Oliver's body was dug up and hung at Tyburn in London. His head was then cut off and put on a pole while his body was thrown into a pit. The head later found it's way into various hands and finally, in this century, was buried in the grounds of his old college at Cambridge.

After Oliver's death, Royalist propaganda tried to blacken Cromwell's name by calling him everything from a kill-joy puritan to crazed dictator. Gradually people saw through these lies and even as early as 1667, Samuel Pepys wrote of him 'Everybody do nowadays reflect upon Oliver and commend him what brave things he did and made all the neighbour Princes fear him'. Today Oliver is regarded by most as a great leader and statesman. His achievements at home were vast and varied and it would be impossible to list them all here. He proved himself a military genius and treated his soldiers with respect, forming them into the greatest fighting force of their day. His rule as Lord Protector gave England peace and security after much troubled times. Scotland, Ireland, and England were united, some religious tolerance was introduced, new schools were founded, and grants were given to promote education, the harsh prison system was improved and made more humane, cruel sports such as cock fighting and bear baiting were banned. The Arts were encouraged and painting and music flourished; the first English Opera was performed and women took to the stage for the first time. Scientific study increased and trade and commerce made the Commonwealth prosperous and wealthy, while law and order were maintained thoughout the Land. Abroad his achievements were even greater and he was respected thoughout Europe. His reformed Navy cleared the Mediterranean of pirates and, under him., the Commonwealth acquired new colonies abroad. In Jamaica he freed the Indians from the horrors of the Spanish Inquisition and the Navy, under Admiral Blake, defeated the Spaniards, thus ending their days as a major world power.

His Commonwealth signed trade treaties with Holland, Sweden, and Denmark and acquired Dunkirk from the French in gratitude for Oliver's alliance with them to defeat the Spaniards. Oliver's Navy made Britain the strongest sea power in Europe and laid the foundations for the British Empire. His far-sighted policies made Britain great at home and abroad and even the Royalist historian, Clarendon, was forced to admit that Oliver's foreign policies were 'magnanimous, enterprising, and successful'. All this was the more amazing by the fact that Oliver had only ruled for five years and had no former experience of power such as this.

But what of Oliver the Man? In appearance he was just under six feet tall and had long brown hair with grey-blue eyes and with a thick-set ruddy complexion. He was not a vain man and once told a painter to paint him 'warts and everything'. He was devoted to

A STILL YOUTHFUL OLIVER IN THE 1640S

CROMWELL IN 1658

Age and responsibilities leave their mark.

his wife and family and after 30 years of marriage wrote to her 'Thou art dearer to me that any creature'. Oliver was also a man of great humour and, during the Civil War, would often laugh and joke with his soldiers. He also enjoyed pranks and it is recorded that once, during a serious meeting with some friends, Oliver started a pillow fight. He liked to dress simply and his diet consisted of plain, substantial dishes, although he enjoyed ale and sometimes a glass of wine.

For his recreation Oliver enjoyed outdoor sports and often played bowls and went hawking and riding. He was never a stern puritan or bigot and indeed loved music, singing, and dancing. He had an organ introduced into Hampton Court and would often sit and listen to the poet, John Milton, playing it. Masques and dances were also regularly held at Hampton and it is recorded once that Oliver had a non-singing part in one of these. He would often use large amounts of money for charity and record states this may have been, sometimes, as much as £40,000 a year. Oliver never ceased to love his God and was a man of great humility, tolerance, and sincerity. He would always listen to critics of his policies and hear their point of view, arguing his case to them freely.. His introduction of religious tolerance was far ahead of it's time, although sadly at the return lf Charles II, this was reversed and religious persecution was brought back.

Oliver Cromwell had never been an ambitious man and only accepted the position of Lord Protector after two Parliaments had failed, due to their constant bickering amongst themselves. Oliver's dream was for 'a land fit for everyone to live in peace and security' and, up until his death, he never ceased from that quest. He lived and died for his Country and it was a great tragedy that everything he had worked for was thrown away when the so-called Restoration occurred. For in the words of the historian Lord Shelbourne, 'while he had power . . . (he) did more set things forward that all the Kings who reigned during that century, England was never so much respected abroad while at home . . . talents of every kind began to show themselves, which were immediately put to sleep or crushed at the Restoration'.

If any man deserves the title of the Greatest Englishman, then it is certainly him and the final words on Oliver best belong to his former servant, John Maidston, 'A larger soul hath seldom dwelt in a house of clay'.

CROMWELL DRESSED IN FULL IMPERIAL ROBES LIES IN STATE AT SOMERSET HOUSE

PLACES TO VISIT OF CIVIL WAR INTEREST IN GAINSBOROUGH

THE BATTLEFIELD

AFTER THE CIVIL WAR, Gainsborough prospered, gradually expanded and, over the years, started to encroach upon the area of the battle site. Today, the main battle site at Foxby Hill, overlooking Sandsfield Lane where Cromwell and Meldrum clashed with Cavendish's forces, is still relatively free of development. Most of the hill remains open grassland and trees although some parts of it have now become school playing fields, and the south end is bisected by Foxby Road. The best place to view the battle site is from the south end of Sandsfield Lane near Foxby Road where, above the lane, the battlefield can be seen dotted with shrubs and trees. Just south of Foxby Road the hill slopes down to Lea Road and this is where Cromwell and Meldrum would have advanced up to meet the Royalists drawn up on the summit of the hill. Due west of here on the far side of Humble Carr Lane next to the River Trent, lies Candish Bog, where the remaining Royalists and their leader fled in panic after being defeated and where Cavendish was struck down and killed. The area is now private property and has all but disappeared under modern mill buildings.

Today, in Gainsborough, the only memories of the battle are recorded in some of the street names thereabouts. There is a Cromwell Avenue and Cromwell Street as well as a Cavendish Drive, and at the junction of Tooley Street and Trinity Street lies a late 19th Century house which is named after Cromwell. Unfortunately, at the present time, these are the only memorials to the battle and it is surely time that Gainsborough Council erected a commemorative plaque to this small, but important, Civil War conflict, which represents a bloody and violent period of Gainsborough's historic past.

GAINSBOROUGH OLD HALL – PARNELL STREET

GAINSBOROUGH OLD HALL lies in the centre of the town and looks much the same as it did when the Civil War was being fought. The house is one of the best preserved mediaeval manor houses in Britain and was first built by Sir Thomas Burgh in the late 15th Century. In the 'Wars of the Roses' Sir Thomas survived by astutely changing sides to support the reigning monarch of the day. He built this house between 1460 and c. 1490, adding to it as his career flourished. Both Richard III and Henry VIII stayed there. The Burgh family remained at the Hall until 1596 when they sold it to the Hickman Family. At the outbreak of Civil War, the head of the family was Willoughby Hickman, who was related to some of the most prominent Puritan families in Lincolnshire as well as being the nephew of Lord Willoughby of Parham, who was later to attack and occupy the town. Hickman became a commissioner for raising parliamentary funds, although in November 1643, while Gainsborough was in Royalist hands, he accepted a baronetcy from Charles I. Despite protests, he was now regarded as a Royalist and, after the Civil War, was fined £1000 by Parliament, although this was later reduced to £50 due to the fact that his income came from market tolls and other dependent estates. Willoughby died in 1650 with his son William taking over the estates, During Cromwell's rule, William allowed secret Royalist meetings to be held at the Hall and, after the return of the Monarchy in 1660, he was rewarded for his Royalist sympathies by becoming MP for East Retford in the Royalist Parliament and obtaining other Crown offices from a grateful Charles II.

The Hickmans moved in 1720 and since then the Hall has been used for a variety of purposes including a public house, linen factory, theatre, and church. Today it is managed jointly by the Lincolnshire County Council and English Heritage. The Hall contains many interesting features including a mediæval kitchen

GAINSBOROUGH OLD HALL FROM A PRINT OF 1817.

with the recreation of a scene of 1483. The Great Hall, the hub of the household, and two rooms are furnished in the style of the 17th Century with several examples of period furniture. There are also displays on Richard III, Henry VIII and the Pilgrim Fathers, those Separatists who left England due to religious persecution by James I. Members of the Separatist Church had met here regularly in the early years of the 17th Century and, indeed, some of its members later sailed in the Mayflower.

OPENING TIMES

EASTER TO OCTOBER		NOVEMBER TO EASTER
Mon. – Sat.	10.00 a.m. – 5.00 p.m.	Mon. – Sat. 10.00 a.m. – 5.00 p.m.
Sun.	2.00 p.m. – 5.30 p.m.	

ALL SAINTS CHURCH, CHURCH STREET

ALL SAINTS' CHURCH AS IT APPEARED DURING THE CIVIL WAR.

A CHURCH has stood on this site since at least 1185 although all that remains from Cromwell's day is the late 14th century tower which houses eight bells. It is constructed in the architectural style known as perpendicular with battlemented and pinnacled crown and imposing traceried windows. The rest of the church was rebuilt in the 18th century in the neo-classical style. It has a central aisle flanked by box pews leading to an apse at the east end together with fine Corinthian columns supporting a plaster roof and balconies. During the Civil War, several Puritan Parliamentarian supporters refused to attend the church services here and, as a result, were regularly excommunicated. Also at this time the parish burial register records the burial of several inhabitants killed during the fighting together with the burial of a number of soldiers.

OPENING TIMES
EVERY DAY: 10.00 a.m. — 4.00 p.m